Apostolic and Prophetic Foundations 101

Apostolic and Prophetic Foundations 101
*

Foundational Studies for the Apostolic and Prophetic Ministries

Roderick L. Evans

CAMDEN, NORTH CAROLINA

Apostolic and Prophetic Foundations 101
Foundational Studies for the Apostolic and Prophetic Ministries

All Rights reserved © 2009 by Roderick L. Evans

No part of this book may be reproduced or transmitted in any form or by any means, graphic, electronic, or mechanical, including photocopying, recording, taping, or by any information storage or retrieval system, without the permission in writing from the publisher.

Front & Back Cover Designs by Kingdom Builders Publishing
All rights reserved.

Kingdom Builders Publishing
an imprint of Kingdom Builders International Ministries

For information address:
Kingdom Builders International
P.O. Box 126
Camden, NC 27921

Unless otherwise indicated, all of the scripture quotations are taken from the *Authorized King James Version* of the Bible. Scripture quotations marked with NIV are taken from the *New International Version* of the Bible. Scripture quotations marked with NASV are taken from the *New American Standard Version* of the Bible. Scripture quotations marked with Amplified are taken from the *Amplified Bible*.

ISBN 13: 978-1-60141-144-0

Printed in the United States of America

Contents

Introduction

Lesson I – No Other Foundation   **1**

Foundation of Old Covenant   *2*
Foundation of New Covenant   *4*
Foundation of the Church   *6*

Lesson II – The Apostolic Office   **11**

Characteristics of an Apostle   *12*
Apostolic Character   *15*
Nine Functions of the Apostle   *17*
Misconceptions   *20*

Lesson III – The Prophetic Office   **27**

Characteristics of a Prophet   *28*
Prophetic Character   *31*
Nine Functions of the Prophetic Office   *34*
Misconceptions   *36*

Lesson IV – Apostles & Prophets   **41**

Similarities of the Offices   *41*
Differences of the Offices   *42*
How the Offices Work Together   *44*

Lesson V – Apostles & Prophets in Perspective — 49

Apostles, Prophets, and the Church — 49
Apostles, Prophets, and Pastors — 52
Apostles versus Prophets — 54

Lesson VI – Apostolic & Prophetic Goals — 57

Focus of the Apostolic Anointing — 57
Focus of the Prophetic Anointing — 58
Apostolic and Prophetic Together — 59

Lesson VII – Understanding "Anointings" — 63

Anointings in the Old Testament — 63
Anointings in the New Testament — 65
Office versus Anointing — 68

Lesson VIII – The Apostolic Anointing — 73

Characteristics of Apostolic People — 74
Character Traits of Apostolic People — 77
Recognizing the Apostolic Anointing — 79
Flowing in the Apostolic Anointing — 81

Lesson IX – The Prophetic Anointing — 85

Characteristics of Prophetic People — 85
Character Traits of Prophetic People — 88
Identifying the Prophetic Anointing — 90
Walking in the Prophetic Anointing — 92

About the Ministry

Other Study Series Publications

Lesson 1 – No Other Foundation

The most important part of any building is the foundation. Any part of a building may be changed at any time, but the foundation must be solid. Walls, ceiling, and fixtures are exchanged frequently, but the foundation must be created to last. God is the ultimate architect. Through His spoken word, He created the universe and the world (Genesis 1:1-30).

__Through faith we understand that the worlds were framed by the (spoken) word of God, so that things which are seen were not made of things which do appear (Hebrews 11: 3, Parentheses mine)__

Whenever He wanted to establish relationship with man, He always laid a foundation for man to build upon. Even in the Garden of Eden, His relationship with man was established on the foundation that they would not eat of the tree of the knowledge of good and evil.

__And the Lord God commanded the man, saying, Of every tree of the garden thou mayest freely eat: But of the tree of the knowledge of good and evil, thou shalt not eat of it: for in the day that thou eatest thereof thou shalt surely die (Genesis 2:16-17).__

When man no longer gave respect unto the foundation, but weakened it through disobedience, God had to once again lay another foundation for man to come into covenant with Him.

FOUNDATION OF THE OLD COVENANT

And Moses brought forth the people out of the camp to meet with God; and they stood at the nether part of the mount (Exodus 19:17).

From Adam to Moses, there was no set law or foundation for man to interact with God. After Israel was freed from Egyptian bondage, God laid the foundation for what is referred to now as the Old Covenant or Testament. At Mount Sinai, God gathered the people together to lay the foundation for the Old Covenant. The Old Covenant was founded upon the Law. The Law was a set a rules and regulations that governed all the major aspects of man's life. The Law covered these major areas:

1) Man's relationship with God
2) Man's relationship with one another
3) Man's religious worship of God

At the core of the Law were the Ten Commandments. From Exodus chapter 20, we discover these ten edicts:

> a. **Do not serve/worship any other Gods (verses 1-3)**
> b. **Do not make any graven images (verses 4-6)**
> c. **Do not use His name in vain (verse 7)**
> d. **Observe the Sabbath Day (verses 8-11)**
> e. **Respect/Honor your parents (verse 12)**

f. Do not kill (verse 13)
g. Do not commit adultery (verse 14)
h. Do not steal (verse 15)
i. Do not lie (verse 16)
j. Do not covet or lust (verse 17)

We learn, however, that Israel could not keep the commandments and they continually rebelled and sinned against God. Israel reduced the worship of God from relationship into ritual. In addition, the Bible teaches that the Old Covenant failed, because it was founded upon principles that could do nothing for the heart and conscience of man.

> ***Seeing that that first [outer portion of the] tabernacle was a parable – a visible symbol or type or picture of the present age. In it gifts and sacrifices are offered, and yet are incapable of perfecting the conscience and renewing the inner man of the worshipper (Hebrews 9:9 Amplified).***

Even though there were religious sects, such as the Pharisees and Sadducees, who adhered to Law in its strictest since, still missed the righteousness of God and failed to respond to Him properly.

> ***For they (Pharisees & Sadducees) being ignorant of God's righteousness, and going about to establish their own righteousness, have not submitted themselves unto the righteousness of God (Romans 10:3, Parentheses mine).***

Therefore, God rejected them and their nation and sought to

establish another covenant. In order to do this, He needed a new foundation for this new covenant.

FOUNDATION OF THE NEW COVENANT

The Old Covenant failed and God decided to establish another covenant. Unlike the old covenant, which was founded upon laws and principles, this new covenant would be founded upon a person. God sent Christ into the world not only to help mankind to take part in the new covenant, but also to be the very foundation for it.

> ***For God so loved the world, that he gave his only begotten Son, that whosoever believeth in him should not perish, but have everlasting life (John 3:16).***
>
> ***For no man can lay a foundation other than the one which is laid, which is Jesus Christ (I Corinthians 3:11).***

The New Covenant was founded upon Christ and the work that He did on the cross. God did not give man any more laws and rules to follow, but to believe on Him that was able to fulfill the Law. And then, through the presence of the Spirit of God, man became able to adhere to the principles originally ordained of God from the beginning.

With the establishment of the New Covenant, God's desire for His people to be set aside and separate still remained.

> *Wherefore come out from among them, and be ye separate, saith the Lord, and touch not the unclean thing; and I will receive you. And will be a Father unto you, and ye shall be my sons and daughters, saith the Lord Almighty. (II Corinthians 6:17-18)*

Along with this command, the New Covenant demanded that God be worshipped differently. Worship was to be performed in and through the Holy Spirit and not based upon ritual.

> *God is a Spirit: and they that worship him must worship him in spirit and in truth (John 4:23-24).*

> *But now we are delivered from the law, that being dead wherein we were held; that we should serve in newness of spirit, and not in the oldness of the letter (Romans 7:6).*

Unlike the Old Covenant, God no longer wanted His presence to be confined to a building, but He wanted to dwell in man's heart.

> *For finding fault with them, he saith, Behold, the days come, saith the Lord, when I will make a new covenant with the house of Israel and with the house of Judah: Not according to the covenant that I made with their fathers in the day when I took them by the hand to lead them out of the land of Egypt; because they continued not in my covenant, and I regarded them not, saith the Lord. For this is the covenant that I will make with the house of Israel after those days, saith the Lord; I will put my laws into their mind, and write them in their hearts:*

and I will be to them a God, and they shall be to me a people. (Hebrews 8:8-10)

FOUNDATION OF THE CHURCH

Under the Old Covenant, the presence and worship of God was always associated with the Tabernacle (of Moses in the wilderness) and Temple (built by Solomon). But the New Covenant made the people of God both the tabernacles and temples of God. Most Christians agree that the birth of the Church was on the day of Pentecost.

And when the day of Pentecost was fully come, they were all with one accord in one place. And suddenly there came a sound from heaven as of a rushing mighty wind, and it filled all the house where they were sitting. And there appeared unto them cloven tongues like as of fire, and it sat upon each of them. And they were all filled with the Holy Ghost, and began to speak with other tongues, as the Spirit gave them utterance. (Acts 2:1-4)

On the day of Pentecost, God made it clear that His temple would be the believer. As He dwells in each one, when they join together they corporately become the temple of God.

*Ye also, as lively stones, are built up a spiritual house, an holy priesthood, to offer up spiritual sacrifices, acceptable to God by Jesus Christ.
(I Peter 2:5)*

> *What? Know ye not that your body is the temple of the Holy Ghost which is in you, which ye have of God, and ye are not your own?*
> *(I Corinthians 6:19)*

The New Covenant Church consists of people, therefore it is understood that the foundation of the Church would also consist of people. As Paul wrote to the believers, he told them a very important truth. They (The Church) were built upon the foundation of the apostles and prophets with Christ being the chief stone.

> *Now therefore ye are no more strangers and foreigners, but fellowcitizens with the saints, and of the household of God; And are built upon the foundation of the apostles and prophets, Jesus Christ himself being the chief corner stone; In whom all the building fitly framed together groweth unto an holy temple in the Lord: In whom ye also are builded together for an habitation of God through the Spirit. (Ephesians 2:19-22)*

From the above verses, we learn some valuable truths about the Church.

1) **The Church is founded upon people, namely the apostles and prophets with Christ being the Head.**
2) **God allowed His people to have a more active role in the establishing of the worship, doctrine, and protocol.**
3) **As directed by Christ through the Spirit, the responsibility for the Church rested upon those early day apostles and prophets.**

When God established the Old Covenant, He told Moses everything that he should write. When it came to the tabernacle, He gave Him specific instructions on how to build it.

> *Who serve unto the example and shadow of heavenly things, as Moses was admonished of God when he was about to make the tabernacle: for, See, saith he, that thou make all things according to the pattern shewed to thee in the mount. (Hebrews 8:5)*

With the Church, God never gave us a specific way to worship Him. He only commanded that it be done in the Spirit and in order (I Corinthians 14:40). This is the reason why there are many denominations and various ways of worship in the New Testament Church. He came to free us from legalistic worship void of His presence and power.

If Christ's ministry to the Church never ended, then we know that the ministries of apostles and prophets to the Church have not ended either. They are all a part of the foundation of the Church. We must go on to understand these ministry offices and the anointing that they carry in order for us to be a healthy Church.

Questions:

1) What was the God's covenant with man in the Garden founded upon?
2) What was the Old Covenant founded upon?
3) Why did the first covenant fail?
4) Who/What is the foundation for the New Covenant?

5) What makes up the foundation for the Church?
6) Who/What/Where is the "Temple" of God under the New Covenant?
7) Have you ever doubted the existence of apostles and prophets? Why?

Notes:

Apostolic and Prophetic Foundations 101: Foundational Studies for the Apostolic and Prophetic Ministries

Lesson 2 – The Apostolic Office

The first ministry to be on display in the New Testament Church was that of the apostle. The Book of Acts highlights the ministry of the apostles. Some biblical scholars have asserted that the only true apostles were the eleven (excluding Judas Iscariot) with the exception of Paul.

Others have stated that the ministry of the apostles is useless since we have the canon of scripture. In addition, others promote that apostolic ministry ceased after the deaths of the first century apostles. All of these teachings are erroneous.

The ministry of the apostle is still vital and important to the advancement of the kingdom of God and the Church. Without this ministry, the Church cannot fulfill its mission in the earth.

Apostle – In the Greek it is *apostolos,* means one who is sent

> *1) Apostles are sent from the presence of God with a divine message.*
>
> *2) Apostles are sent to perform a specific task.*
>
> *3) Apostles will execute their duties in different manner.*
>
> *4) Apostles will have different anointing.*
>
> *5) Apostles will have different ministries. (I Corinthians 12:4-6)*

CHARACTERISTICS OF AN APOSTLE

Apostolic ministry manifests itself in various ways. However, there is some common ground among all apostles. No matter what their specific calls are, apostles will exhibit characteristics of ambassadors, fathers, and husbands as they minister in the Church.

Apostles as Ambassadors (II Corinthians 5:20, Amplified)

Paul compared the apostle's ministry to that of an ambassador.

1) Ambassadors are the highest officials/representatives in government. The word translated ambassador "presbeuo" means senior representative. The apostle is the senior representative of the kingdom of God.

2) Ambassadors are sent forth with specific guidelines of the one who sent them. An ambassador's duty is assigned to him. Apostles cannot choose how they will operate in ministry. God decides it.

3) Ambassador's influence is limited to that given by ruler or government. An ambassador only has influence in the countries given him by his leader. Apostles have authority over what God gives them. They cannot assume leadership over anyone or anything because they are apostles.

4) Ambassadors words are equal to the one that sent them. When ambassadors are commissioned, they are to speak in the stead of their leaders. Apostles are to represent the voice of Christ as they minister in the Church.

5) Ambassadors have an invested/inherent authority. Ambassadors are sent with all authority and power of the commissioning government. Apostles are sent to minister in the authority of Christ. However, their authority originates with the will of God.

6) Ambassadors are expected to have wisdom, counsel, and knowledge of their ruler. Ambassadors have to represent their government in integrity, knowledge, and wisdom. Apostles, too, must possess the wisdom and knowledge of Christ.

Apostles as Fathers (I Corinthians 4:15; I John 2:1)

Apostles are to serve as a "father" ministry in the Church also. Paul and John likened their relationship to the people of God to a father-child relationship.

1) Fathers provide for their children (II Corinthians 12:14-15). The apostle will supply the spiritual needs of those entrusted to him.

2) Fathers nurture their children (I Thessalonians 2:7). The apostle's concern for the Church will be a personal one.

3) Fathers discipline their children (II Cor. 5:1-5). Apostles will execute judgment, discipline, and correction in the Church.

4) Fathers give wise/sound instruction to their children (Acts 2:42; Jude 17). Apostles will impart revelation and knowledge to the Church as a father does to his children.

Apostles as Husbands (Ephesians 5:22-32; I Peter 3:7)

Since apostles stand in Christ's stead, it is imperative to understand that the Christ-Church relationship is compared to a marriage. The apostles are married to the Church and function in the Church as a husband in a marriage. Ephesians gives guidelines for marriage; the same applies to the apostolic ministry in the Church.

1) Husbands must love their wives (I Corinthians 4:9-10). Apostles have a deep love for the Church. They minister in the Church with the love and compassion of Christ.

2) Husbands must impart the Word to wives (John 15:3; II Corinthians 11:2). As husbands to the Church, apostles share in the responsibility of cleansing the Church through the Word. The reason is to present the Church unto God without spot or wrinkle.

3) Husbands must love their wives as their own bodies. Apostles have to minister with great love. Though they minister to the Church, they themselves are also a part of the Church. In the end, the apostles and the Church will stand before the judgment seat of God.

APOSTOLIC CHARACTER

As ambassadors, fathers, and husbands, apostles reflect the very nature of Christ and God. The apostle's ministry is not only based upon what he does (which is subjective to the will of God), but also in who he is. Mature apostles are known primarily by their godly characters, and secondarily by their ministries.

The apostle's character finds its definition within the person of Christ. To fully represent Christ, the apostle's character has to be fashioned according to the fruit of the Spirit.

> *But the fruit of the Spirit is love, joy, peace, patience, kindness, goodness, faithfulness, gentleness, self-control; against such there is no law. (Galatians 5:22-23)*

The fruit of the spirit then becomes the "fruit of apostolic character."

1) Love – Apostles have to have an everlasting love for God, the Church, and their family. (I Corinthians 13:4-7)

2) Joy – Apostles possess the message of the kingdom of God. Part of that message is joy. Apostles must have joy and promote joy. (Romans 14:7)

3) Peace – Apostles have to be ministers of peace. They have to inspire peace in the Church and remind them of the Christ-given peace. (John 14:27)

4) Patience – Patience is the hallmark of true apostolic ministry. Patience brings balance to their purpose driven ministries. (II Corinthians 12:12)

5) Kindness – Apostles have to be kind. Apostles have no excuse to be rude or mean, even though they exercise authority in the Spirit. (Titus 1:8)

6) Goodness – Good deeds must accompany the apostles' ministries. They have to be godly in their interaction with the saints. (Galatians 6:10)

7) Faithfulness – Every apostle must have the character trait of faithfulness. Apostles have to be faithful to God and their ministries to the Church. (I Corinthians 4:1-2)

8) Gentleness – Apostles have to gentle as they minister to the saints and interact with friends and family. It is a required trait for the servant of the Lord.
(II Timothy 2:24)

9) Self-control – Apostles are to exercise self-control in every affair of their lives: whether in the pulpit, on the mission field, or in their homes. (Titus 1:7-8)

Anyone called to the apostolic ministry must remember that success in ministry is not in ministerial activities, but the maintenance of character, integrity, and conduct.

NINE FUNCTIONS OF THE APOSTOLIC OFFICE

Though there are varieties of ministries and operations, most apostles will demonstrate most or all of these functions.

I. Preach/Teach Word of God (I Cor. 4:1; I Tim. 2:7)

Every apostle is gifted to preach or teach the Word of God. They will do it under divine inspiration. They are anointed to make known unto the Church the mysteries of God through the Word. This is performed with clarity and accuracy.

II. Impart Spiritual Gifts (Acts 8:17; Romans 1:11; II Tim. 1:6; I Tim. 4:14)

Apostles have the ability to bring forth gifts of God in the lives of believers. They have the ability to impart wisdom, knowledge, and understanding. Apostles can bring to light spiritual gifts resident in believers and impart gifts (by the direction of the Spirit) through the laying on of hands.

III. Establish & Oversee Churches/Organizations (Acts 15:3; 15:36)

Because apostles are sent with a divine message, God will use some of them to start organizations as vehicles to present their message. In addition, apostles will start new churches and ministries in areas where they have ministered the Word of the Lord. This is to give structure to those who hear their message.

IV. Evangelize (Acts 13:47; Galatians 2:7-8)

Every apostle has a message. They are gifted in going into areas that have not been open to the gospel. Jesus sent the original apostles out to preach. Every apostle will function as an evangelist, whether to the Church (to bring balance and order) or to the lost (for redemption and salvation).

V. Raise up Leaders (II Timothy 2:1-2; Acts 15:39; Titus 1:4-5; Acts 6:3-6)

Because of the authority given them, apostles have the anointing and responsibility to raise up leaders. This will be done for the further advancement of the Kingdom of God. Apostles will have "Timothys" and "Elishas" in ministry so that when they are gone, the work will go on. If apostles are heads of ministries, they will have the ability to recognize gifts and ministries in the people and set them in the Church as directed by the Spirit.

VI. Expose False Apostles/Doctrine (II Tim. 2:17; II Peter 2:1; II Cor. 11:13)

Apostles are stewards of the mysteries of God. They have the wisdom and foresight to warn against deception. They will contend for purity of faith and doctrine in the Church. They, like prophets of old, will warn and speak against false apostles openly.

VII. Perform Signs, Wonders, Healings, Miracles (Acts 2:43, 4:33; Acts 8:23; Acts 13:11)

The apostle has a miraculous ministry. Apostles are gifted

men, not only to work signs and wonders, but also in the other gifts of the spirit. The word of knowledge, the word of wisdom, discerning of spirits, and prophecy will operate regularly in their ministries.

VIII. Lay Spiritual Foundation in Church (Acts 15:28; I Cor. 3:10; Eph. 2:20, 3:5)

Apostles have the authority and anointing to lay spiritual foundations in the Church. Though no modern-day apostles will write scripture, they are equipped to reveal hidden truths of God's Word and lay foundations for the people of God to grow thereby.

IX. Establish Churches in the Faith (Gospel) (Acts 16:5, Galatians 1:6; Jude 1:3)

Apostles have the unique ability to bring the people back to the purity of the faith. They have the ability to instruct babes in Christ; that they may become mature in their walks and in their doctrine. They have the ability to promote growth and stability in the Body of Christ.

Though there are many dimensions to this awesome ministry (not listed), most apostles will demonstrate all of these functions at some time in their ministries.

We will now examine erroneous misconceptions and beliefs about apostles.

MISCONCEPTIONS

I. Paul is not the standard for all apostles (Galatians 2:7-8 NIV)

One mistake that Christian theologians have made is to make the ministry of Paul the standard for all apostles. Scholars infer that Paul is the barometer for all apostles because his ministry is highlighted more than others.

However, God operates in diversity even among those with the same ministry. Though Peter and Paul were apostles, Galatians informs us that they did not minister to the same group, or in the same manner.

II. Not all apostles will do evangelistic work, though they will be involved (Acts 15:22)

In the scriptures, we read of apostles like Peter, Paul, Barnabas, and Apollos who traveled frequently and ministered. However, other apostles were stationary like James and the other apostles located in Jerusalem.

The scriptures give no indication that these men traveled extensively, but numerous accounts are given of these men sending emissaries to monitor the growth of the Church. Among those sent from them were Paul, Barnabas, Judas and Silas, Agabus and other prophets, and Peter.

III. Not all apostles will start churches (II Corinthians 9:1; 12:12)

Because of the ministry of Paul and Barnabas, it has become the rule that apostles will start churches. James, who exercised oversight in Jerusalem, did not start the work there. Paul and Barnabas had to start churches in order to give the Gentiles an order for the worship of God.

They went in areas where Christ was not preached. Therefore, they had to start churches and appoint leaders. Please remember, a sign of the apostolic anointing is the starting of churches and organizations, but it is not mandatory.

The scriptures give no indication that this is a qualification to be an apostle. If we hold to this belief, we would have to call every leader that has started a church, organization, or ministry, an apostle. We know that this is not true. The qualification for apostolic ministry is based upon godly attributes and power.

IV. An apostle is not an apostle over all (Romans 15:20; I Corinthians 9:2)

Some immature apostles and leaders have promoted the doctrine that if someone is an apostle; they exercise apostolic authority over any church they choose. This is not true. An apostle is only an apostle where he is received as an apostle or appointed or anointed/appointed by God.

Paul did not preach the gospel where any others had preached Christ and he only exercised apostolic oversight over churches he established. He was given apostolic oversight over churches he did not start, at their request (Colossians 2:1)

V. Local churches do not need to be under an apostle's ministry (Acts 13:1-3)

It is true that any church that receives an apostle or is under a true apostle's ministry will be greatly blessed. However, there were numerous churches in the apostle's day that was not under apostolic control. The church at Antioch was started after the saints fled persecution (Acts 11:19). The elders at Jerusalem sent Paul and Barnabas to check on the work, not to take control.

The Jerusalem apostles and elders did not replace the leadership with their own elders. They left the church in the hands of those who began it. In addition, we find that at the church of Antioch, no apostles were named. Only prophets and teachers seemed to exercise rule and authority. We discover that these leaders were intricate in launching Paul and Barnabas into the apostolic ministry.

VI. An apostle does not have to function in another ministry before operating in apostolic ministry.

With the acceptance of apostles came this restriction: To operate in apostolic ministry, one must first operate in another one of the ministry offices. It is true that some apostles operated in other ministries before they became apostles, this was the case with Paul and Barnabas. In Antioch, Paul (Saul) and Barnabas were listed among the prophets and teachers.

There are apostles, today, who have operated for years as prophets, evangelists, and pastors before God released them into the greater work. God used the other offices as their training. It will enhance the apostolic ministry in them.

If someone can teach, evangelize, pastor, and be a prophet without operating in another ministry, the same holds true for the apostle. We read of men like James, Jude, and Apollos who were of note among the apostles without having operated in another capacity in the Church. Timothy and Titus were under Paul's instruction and then they were released into apostolic ministry to the churches where he sent them.

VII. Apostles are not exempt from accountability and Church authority (Galatians 2:2, 11, 14; I Timothy 5:20)

Apostles are not to be their own boss. If they are heads of organizations, then they need to be in fellowship and accountability with other leaders. Also, if an apostle is not the overseer over a church, but has ministry; he must be submitted to a local church and governing body as any other saint. Apostles are not above rebuke, correction, and discipline. Peter was rebuked by Paul.

If someone is an apostle and the pastor is not, the apostolic minister is not above the local leader. The pastor is his head and he must be submitted to him. Paul submitted his ministry to the leadership in Jerusalem for counsel.

Now that we have discussed the characteristics of an apostle, apostolic character, the functions of an apostle, and misconceptions about apostolic ministry, let us examine the prophetic office.

QUESTIONS:

1. What is an apostle?
2. In what ways is an apostle like an ambassador? A father? A husband?
3. Do you know any individuals who exhibit many of these qualities?
4. What are the fruit of the Spirit?
5. Why is it important for apostles to have godly character?
6. How does godly character enhance the apostle's ministry?
7. What could be the results of an apostle lacking the fruit of the Spirit?
8. Discuss, in brief, the functions of an apostle.
9. Do you know of anyone whom you would consider a modern-day apostle?
10. Discuss misconceptions surrounding the apostolic office.
11. Why do you think misconceptions are accepted?

Notes:
_____
_____
_____
_____
_____

Lesson 3 – The Prophetic Office

The prophets are here! God always spoke to His people through the ministry of the prophets. After the Church was established, prophets continued to minister. The ministry of prophets did not cease after the deaths of the first century apostles and prophets.

Some scholars have promoted the idea that since we have scripture, there is no need for prophetic ministry. Others believe that since the Holy Spirit is in all believers, individuals can hear from God without the ministry of the prophets. However, we should know that these doctrines are incorrect.

Prophets and prophetic ministry are essential to God's purpose for the Church. God established this ministry in the Church second only to apostolic ministry.

And, God hath set some in the church, first apostles, secondarily prophets… (I Corinthians 12:28)

Prophet – Greek term "*prophetes*" – means an inspired speaker, a foreteller

1) Prophets only speak for God

2) Prophets communicate the heart and mind of God

3) Prophets are unique in their ministries

4) Prophets are set aside for God alone

CHARACTERISTICS OF A PROPHET

All prophets are not the same. However, there are certain characteristics that prophets will possess. All prophets exhibit characteristics of messengers and interpreters.

Prophets as Messengers

1) Messengers are deliverers of the sender's message (Ezekiel 3:27)

A messenger's only task is to carry the message from the sender to the recipient. God calls prophets to deliver the Word (message) of the Lord. Though they may function in other areas in ministry, this is their primary task.

2) Messengers are responsible for the message they carry (Ezekiel 33:7)

Messengers have to be careful not to lose or damage the message given them. Some messengers have to deliver oral messages as well as written. Prophets are responsible for the Word that God will give them.

3) Messengers must not alter the message given (Jeremiah 23:28)

Messengers have to be careful to deliver the given message only.

The messenger has to be careful not to tamper with the message in any way. Likewise, prophets have to deliver the Word as God gives it to them. They should not alter the message because of personal opinion/bias, popularity, or gain.

4) Messengers have to be fearless (Jeremiah 1:8)

Messengers have been killed for the message they delivered. Throughout history, there are numerous stories of messengers who are killed for relaying another's message. Therefore, a messenger has to be fearless. Prophets have to be bold in their ministries. There is no place for fear in the life of a prophet. Prophets must deliver the message that God gives in spite of the consequences.

5) Messengers have to be trustworthy (Amos 3:7)

A messenger has to have the trust of the one who sends him. The messenger is the link between the sender and recipient. Thus, he has to be trusted in order to have such a responsibility. The Lord entrusts prophets with His Word. Prophets are to possess integrity. They have to be faithful to their ministries.

Prophets as Interpreters

Important to any kingdom are interpreters. Interpreters are there to help foreign nations understand the messages of the sending governments and ambassadors.

1) Interpreters are important to any kingdom

Interpreters are a valuable resource to any kingdom. They provide nations with the opportunity to communicate with one another without confusion. Prophets have always been an important part of the plan of God in the earth. In the Old Testament, God used prophets to reveal His counsel. In the Church, prophets play an important role in the revelation of Christ to the world.

2) Interpreters understand more than one language

Interpreters have the important task of establishing communication between people of different nationalities and languages. Prophets understand the various manners in which God speaks. They are skilled interpreters of dreams, visions, signs, and events. Prophets have the awesome responsibility to make known unto man the counsel of an invisible God. Prophets are involved in establishing communication between God and man.

3) Interpreters are skilled in communication

Interpreters are more than translators. It is a known fact that it is possible to lose meaning through literal translation. Therefore, it is imperative that the interpreter be able to not only translate, but also communicate the intent of the words spoken. Prophets have to be able to communicate the heart and mind of God as well as the Word of God. They have to communicate His intent for the message.

4) Interpreters do not work alone

When an interpreter is present, he is not the primary communicator. The interpreter's function is secondary to those who are conversing, though vital. Prophets do not work alone. They work aside other ministries to ensure that the counsel of God is understood.

PROPHETIC CHARACTER

Prophets speak for God. The Bible tells us that God is love. Regardless of the message delivered, the prophet's motivation for ministry has to be love. Love should be the foundation for the prophet's character. Love brings balance to the prophets as they deliver messages of rebuke and correction.

I Corinthians 13 gives us a list of the attributes of love. Fifteen traits are listed. Wherever the word "love" is, replace it with "a prophet." If prophets speak the heart of God, the heart of God has to be in them.

> *Love is patient; love is kind. It does not envy; it does not boast; it is not proud. It is not rude; it is not self-seeking; it is not easily angered; it keeps no record of wrongs. Love does not delight in evil but rejoices with the truth. It always protects, always trusts, always hopes, always perseveres. Love never fails. (I Corinthians 13:4-8a)*

1) Patient – Prophets have to be patient. Patience has to govern them as they wait to see the Church act on what God reveals to them.

2) Kind – Prophets have to be nice people. Because they sometimes will speak rebuke and correction, it is no excuse for them to be overbearing and rude.

3) Not envious – Prophets must resist the desire to compete. They should not be envious of another's ministry or position.

4) Not boastful – Prophets hear from God frequently. They have to guard themselves against bragging about their relationship with God.

5) Not proud – Prophets must resist pride at all costs. God gives them great authority in the Spirit realm. However, they should not confuse their spiritual authority with self-worth.

6) Not rude – Prophets have to be courteous in their actions. Ministry is not an excuse for rude behavior.

7) Not self-seeking – Prophets must not use their ministries as platforms for personal gain. They prophesy out of obedience to God, not man.

8) Not easily angered – Prophets can be vulnerable to anger when they feel they are ignored. Prophets have to remember, they represent God. If people do not listen to them, it is not grounds for them to become angry.

9) Keeps no record of wrong – In personal and ministerial life, the prophet has to learn to forgive. Forgiveness is the duty of all believers. However, prophets have to release individuals whom God forgives. Prophets are allowed to see the sins and faults of others. They must learn to release individuals from past sins and not judge.

10) Does not rejoice in evil – Prophets have to guard their hearts against being happy when individuals experience the discipline of God. Jonah hoped for the destruction of Nineveh; he was angered when God had mercy. Prophets have to remember that God's discipline comes because of His love.

11) Rejoices with the truth – Contrary to popular belief, prophets are not to be sad individuals. They should be able to rejoice with the truth, even in adverse settings.

12) Protects – Prophets serve as protectors of the Word of God and the Church. Prophets will guard the Church against false doctrines and spiritual deception.

13) Always trusts – Prophets not only have to trust God, but also fellow believers. Prophets have to resist becoming judgmental of others, using "discernment" as an excuse.

14) Hopes – Prophets are to live by faith and be able to inspire faith in others.

15) Perseveres – Prophets need endurance. They have to persevere through the tests of God, temptations of the devil, trials of men, and the troubles of life.

The gifts and callings of God are without repentance, but the nature of God has to be developed. Because of the spiritual depth of their ministries, prophets need depth of character for balance. Prophets will not fail in their ministries as long as they walk in love.

NINE FUNCTIONS OF THE PROPHETIC OFFICE

Prophetic ministry is multi-faceted. Though there are differences in the administration and demonstration of prophetic gifts, all prophets have essentially the same functions in the Church.

I. Preach/Teach the Word of God (Acts 15:32)

Contrary to popular belief, prophets not only speak under prophetic inspiration, but also expound on the Word of God. Prophets will preach and teach the Word with clarity. The Old Testament prophets proved to be excellent interpreters of the Law; their New Testament counterparts did the same. They will explain hidden mysteries in the Word.

II. Serve as Intercessors (Jeremiah 27:18)

Prophets serve as powerful intercessors. They have burden to see the will of God accomplished. Prophets will pray for extended times and periods.

III. Lay Spiritual Foundations (Ephesians 2:20, 3:5)

Prophets have the authority and anointing to lay spiritual foundations in the Church. Prophets are equipped to reveal hidden truths of God's Word and lay foundations for the people of God to grow thereby.

IV. Reveal/Impart Spiritual Gifts (I Timothy 4:14; Acts 13:1-3)

Prophets have the ability to recognize the gifts of God in believers. They have the ability to impart wisdom, knowledge, and understanding. Prophets can bring to light spiritual gifts resident in believers and impart gifts (by the direction of the Spirit) through the laying on of hands.

V. Prophesy (Ezekiel 3:11; Acts 11:27-28)

Prophets are divinely gifted to prophesy. Their prophecies will be of a greater depth and clarity than other believers who have the gift of prophecy. They will prophesy frequently and accurately. They will have a consistent track record of prophetic words that are true. This is the foundation of their ministry. Though they will intercede, pray, and preach, prophesying is their first priority.

VI. Interpret Signs, Wonders, Dreams, and Visions (Numbers 12:6)

Prophets are gifted to interpret the supernatural manifestations of God. Some are gifted like Daniel in understanding dreams and visions. Others will be able to interpret seemingly natural events through which God is speaking.

VII. Expose False Prophets and Doctrines (Jeremiah 5:31)

Prophets are stewards of the mysteries of God. They have revelation and foresight to warn against spiritual deception. They will contend for purity of faith and doctrine in the Church. They, like prophets of old, will warn and speak against false prophets and ministers, unashamedly.

VIII. Performs Signs, Wonders and Healings (Isaiah 38:7-8)

Prophets will have signs and wonders in their ministry. The signs and wonders will manifest to confirm the spoken prophetic word.

IX. Establish Believers, Churches, and Organizations in the Faith and Will of God (Acts 16:5)

Prophets have the chore to bring the people back to the purity of the faith. They have the ability to promote growth and stability in the Body of Christ. Also, through prophetic insight, they will endeavor to make sure that the plan and will of God is accomplished.

MISCONCEPTIONS

I. Prophets are to be subject to leadership

Prophets are not to override leadership, though they

possess great authority and revelation. If they are not the pastors or heads of the organization, they are not to function outside of the parameters established by the existing leaders. The Old Testament prophets were always subject to the king, though they had to prophesy and cry out against certain activities.

II. Prophets are not to be lone rangers

Prophets are a part of the Body of Christ. The prophets are to function within the community of believers. Some feel that prophets are to be by themselves. This is because they felt that the Old Testament prophets were loners. We understand by the Word that the prophets normally surfaced in groups and some held positions in the government.

III. Revelation must be clear (I Corinthians 14:33)

There are prophets who minister and the individual leaves their presence confused. The revelation of a mature prophet will be clear, for God is not the author of confusion. Prophets declare the word of the Lord. How can the believer obey God if the word is confusing?

IV. Prophets do not always have a word (2 Kings 4:27)

Though God reveals many things to prophets, there are times when God will not give the prophets a word or authorize them to speak a word. Prophets are only prophets when inspired by God to speak.

V. Prophets can be wrong. (I Corinthians 14:29)

Paul told the Corinthians to judge the words given, even by prophets. In both Testaments, prophetic revelation was judged. True prophets may error if they prophesy for gain or out of their own opinions and imaginations..

VI. Prophets can operate in other offices (Acts 2:29-31)

A prophet can operate in another ministry office. We find that Samuel was a priest, prophet, and judge. We find that David was a king and a prophet.

QUESTIONS:

1. *What is a prophet?*
2. *In what ways are prophets like messengers?*
3. *In what ways are prophets like interpreters?*
4. *Name the characteristics of love.*
5. *Why is it important for prophets to have love?*
6. *How does love bring balance to the prophet's ministry?*
7. *What could be the results of a prophet lacking love?*
8. *Name the functions of a prophet.*
9. *Discuss, in brief, the functions of the prophet.*
10. *Discuss prevailing misconceptions surrounding the prophetic office.*
11. *What are some other erroneous beliefs about prophets?*

Notes:

Apostolic and Prophetic Foundations 101: Foundational Studies for the Apostolic and Prophetic Ministries

Lesson 4 - Apostles & Prophets

Since apostles and prophets are foundational to the Church, it is important to understand how these offices work together. In this lesson, we will discover:

1) *The similarities of the offices*
2) *The differences between the offices*
3) *How the offices work together*

There are certain functions and responsibilities that apostles and prophets share. Oftentimes in the demonstration of their ministries, this is clearly seen. Before we can explore the apostolic anointing and the prophetic anointing, it is necessary to know how these offices relate and correlate to one another.

SIMILARITIES BETWEEN THE OFFICES

In lessons 2 and 3, we discovered the nine functions of apostle and of the prophet. From these, we find that apostles and prophets have four functions that each share fully.

1) Preach/Teach the Word

Apostles and prophets share in the responsibility of declaring the gospel of Christ and providing sound doctrine to the Church. Again, prophets have to know the Word and present it with clarity. (Romans 10:14-15)

2) Impart Spiritual Gifts

Each of these ministries has the ability to impart spiritual gifts to believers. Apostles will impart gifts by criteria and need (Titus 1:4-5), while prophets will impart gifts by revelation (Acts 13:1-3).

3) Lay Spiritual Foundations

The ministries of the apostles and the prophets laid the foundation for the Church. No present day apostles and prophets will author scriptures, but they are responsible to make sure that the foundation of Christ stands sure (II Tim. 2:19)

4) Establish Believers & Churches in the Faith

Apostles and prophets have the ability to bring the people back to the purity of the faith. They have the responsibility to promote growth and stability in the Church.

DIFFERENCES OF THE OFFICES

Though there are many similarities between apostles and prophets, there are significant differences also. Apostles and prophets differ in how they relate to the Church. When considering the other functions of the apostles and prophets, we discover the differences.

A) Apostles Evangelize while Prophets Prophesy

Apostles have an evangelistic touch to their ministries. They are sent to a certain group to preach a particular message. Their ministries, like the evangelist, will be to believers and unbelievers. Prophets, however, have to speak only in the name of the Lord. Though God can use them to minister to unbelievers, their ministry is given for the people of God.

B) Apostles Raise up Leaders while Prophets Intercede for Them

Apostles are responsible to train and immobilize leaders in the Church. They are concerned that there are men and women in place to do the work of the Lord. Because of this, apostles have to resist putting immature or unqualified people in positions of authority.

Prophets, conversely, have the responsibility to pray for those in leadership. Though they may reveal gifts and ministries of future leaders, they will serve on the front lines of intercession. Much of their ministry will be to those in leadership positions. Therefore, intercession is one of the hallmarks of prophetic ministry.

C) Apostles Establish Organizations while Prophets Interpret its Vision

Apostles are anointed to start new churches, ministries, and other religious organizations. This is a sign of an apostolic call on an individual's life. Prophets are more concerned that the original vision that God has for a particular church or organization is adhered to. Jesus is the general contractor, the apostles serve as the builders, and the prophets serve as the building inspectors.

D) Apostles and Prophets Expose False Ministers and Doctrine

Apostles and prophets have the ability to recognize false doctrines and ministers. Apostles will have a greater concern for doctrinal purity and organizational stability. Prophets will expose false doctrines and ministers; but they will also focus on exposing false "moves" of God and false anointings. They will endeavor for spiritual purity that divination and familiar spirits will not invade the Church.

Now that we have highlighted the major similarities and differences between apostles and prophets, we can now understand how these offices work together.

HOW THE OFFICES WORK TOGETHER

Since apostles and prophets are foundational to the Church, it is imperative to know how these offices work together. There are two illustrations that describe how apostles and prophets work together in the Church.

    I.   *The illustration of cement and water*
    II.   *The illustration of contractors and inspectors*

These illustrations will bring greater clarity to the offices of the apostle and prophet.

I. The illustration of cement and water

When making concrete for sidewalks and buildings, powdered cement and water are used. Once the cement and water are combined, it is ready to be poured to form pavement and building foundations. Likewise, apostles and prophets work together to form the foundation of the Church. In this illustration, apostolic ministry is comparable to the powdered cement, while prophetic ministry is comparable to the water.

Apostolic ministry is one of substance. Apostles provide stability to the Church. Apostles endeavor for purity of doctrine. They have a great desire for Church organization and structure. This causes some apostles to become legalistic and stagnant. This is where the prophetic ministry becomes vital.

Prophets, conversely, strive to see the Church keep pace with the flow of the Spirit. Prophets bring life to the Church. Water has many uses. Water brings life, cleans, and refreshes. Prophetic ministry should accomplish this in the Church. Prophetic ministry keeps the Church vibrant and clean from spiritual impurity. Prophets prepare the Church for the upcoming moves of God.

Apostles and prophets bring balance to one another. Apostles provide stability for the Church, while prophets facilitate mobility in the Church. Stability and Mobility work together to lay the proper foundation for the Church.

II. The illustration of builders and inspectors

Apostles serve as builders in the Kingdom. Paul compared apostolic ministry to that of a builder.

According to the grace of God, which is given unto me, as a wise master builder, I have laid the foundation, and another buildeth thereon. But let every man take heed how he buildeth thereupon. (I Corinthians 3:10)

Apostles endeavor to lay a spiritual foundation for the saints to grow by. Their ministries provided structure and order for the worship of God. Paul's ministry at Corinth exemplified this. He, along with the other apostles (Peter and Apollos), first laid the foundation for the Church (Christ) and then built upon it through preaching, teaching, and the writing of letters.

However, after the construction of a building, the building inspector's job is important. They come in to ensure that the building is safe for occupancy and that it meets all governmental regulations. The prophet's ministry can be comparable to this. In the Old Testament, the prophets ministered to keep the service and worship of God pure. In the New Testament, the prophet's role remains the same. He is to ensure that the vision of God for any ministry or organization is adhered to.

QUESTIONS:

1. Discuss the similarities between apostles and prophets.
2. Discuss the differences between apostles and prophets.
3. Discuss how they work together.

Notes:

Lesson 5 – Apostles & Prophets in Perspective

The increase of revelation and information opens up the path to deception through excess. As we endeavor to learn more about God and His ministries, we must avoid extremes. History has shown that every time God has moved in the earth, the enemy has tried to counter attack with excess and deception. We see this trend today with the emerging apostolic and prophetic ministries. In this lesson, we will endeavor to bring balance to the numerous teachings surrounding apostles and prophets. In short, we want to keep our outlook on the offices in perspective.

APOSTLES, PROPHETS, AND THE CHURCH

Apostolic and prophetic ministries are foundational ministries in the Church. Foundational does not mean that these ministries are more important or valuable than other ministries. When considering a building, the foundation is not seen. However, when storms and other influences come against the building, the foundation's strength provides support for the building. The same is true for the Church. When apostles and prophets minister properly, they will not be the center of attention, but the entire Church will display the nature of Christ and the power of God.

The true purpose of apostles and prophets is that their ministries help the Church stand against attacks of the enemy and deception. However, we see that the Church has lost vision, purpose, and power. This is because true apostolic and prophetic ministry is missing. Consequently, the Church promotes false doctrines and ministers unwittingly. In addition, it is divided over unimportant issues. The Church has left the simplicity of Christ to follow another gospel, based upon prosperity and not righteousness.

> ***But I fear, lest by any means, as the serpent beguiled Eve through his subtilty, so your minds should be corrupted from the simplicity that is in Christ. For if he that cometh preacheth another Jesus, whom we have not preached, or if ye receive another spirit, which ye have not received, or another gospel, which ye have not accepted, ye might well bear with him. (II Corinthians 11:3-4)***

The error of many apostles and prophets is that they have drawn attention to themselves and their gifts and have neglected their responsibilities to the Church. As a result, the whole Church suffers. Apostles and prophets are to minister so that the Church may shine.

> ***For all things are for your sakes, that the abundant grace might through the thanksgiving of many redound to the glory of God. (II Corinthians 4:15)***

> ***Therefore I endure all things for the elect's sakes, that they may also obtain the salvation which is in Christ Jesus with eternal glory. (II Timothy 2:10)***

Apostles and prophets are to have this mentality as they minister. They minister so the Church would remain partakers of the grace of God unto salvation. The foundation supports the building. When apostles and prophets fulfill their tasks, local assemblies, churches, and organizations are healthy and vibrant.

The problem remains that individuals in the Body of Christ are exalting apostles, prophets, and other ministers above measure in the Church. The Church has to be sober in its acceptance of apostles and prophets. They have to remember that apostles and prophets are men and women redeemed by Christ. Their gifts do not make them special or superior. However, their gifts and ministries make them responsible for the Church. Many apostles and prophets fall into pride and rebellion because men esteem them too highly. What, then, is to be the Church's approach to apostles and prophets?

> ***For I say, through the grace given unto me, to every man that is among you, not to think of himself more highly than he ought to think; but to think soberly, according as God hath dealt to every man the measure of faith. For as we have many members in one body, and all members have not the same office: So we, being many, are one body in Christ, and every one members one of another. (Romans 12:3-5)***

Paul instructed the Romans that they were not to think too much of themselves. However, we must remember not to think too much of apostles and prophets. Why? He goes on to say that God has given every man a measure of faith to operate in whatever ministry or gift he has. Therefore, since God is the source of all gifts, there is no need for the saints to think of anyone too highly. Yet, we are to give respect and honor unto one another as members of Christ.

> ***Render therefore to all their dues: tribute to whom tribute is due; custom to whom custom; fear to whom fear; honour to whom honour. (Romans 13:7)***

Paul told the Romans that they were to give respect unto the leaders in government. Whatever office they held, he told them to give them the respect the office demanded. The same applies to apostles, prophets, and other ministries. We are to respect them for their service in the Lord, especially those who labor for our spiritual well being (this speaks very heavily to pastors).

> ***For if a man think himself to be something, when he is nothing, he deceiveth himself. But let every man prove his own work, and then shall he have rejoicing in himself alone, and not in another. (Galatians 6:3-4)***

Apostles and prophets are not to boast about their labors, for it leads to deception. Conversely, they are to rejoice before the Lord because of the reward He gives.

APOSTLES, PROPHETS, AND PASTORS

The enemy is the author of confusion and division. If he can keep the leaders in the Church divided, they will not minister effectively in the Church. We have already addressed the fact that apostles and prophets are not to think more highly of themselves than they ought. However, since pastors usually have the oversight of local churches and assemblies, there is a need for understanding between apostles, prophets, and pastors.

At the heart of the strife and tension between apostles, prophets, and pastors is the need for control blurred by personal insecurities. When a pastor has an apostle or prophet in his church, he must not allow insecurity and intimidation to grip his spirit. If so, he will perceive everything the apostle or prophet does as a challenge to his authority. Conversely, the apostle or prophet should not try to handle situations reserved for the pastor of the Church. The pastor has the responsibility for the souls of the sheep. He also bears the responsibility for the spiritual oversight of the apostles and prophets that are in fellowship with the assembly.

Oftentimes, the enemy causes a war between pastors and apostles and prophets. The pastors feel intimidated by the manner in which God uses the apostles and prophets, and the apostles and prophets feel that the pastor is against them because of a persecution complex. The need for communication is vital. Without communication, there will be confusion and no one will benefit, but the kingdom of Satan. Pastors have to resist fighting apostles and prophets to feel like they are in control. Control is not the issue, but ministry. However, apostles and prophets have to learn to be subject to leadership if they expect to have fruitful ministries.

All of these ministries are needed in the Body of Christ. Pastors cannot devalue the ministries of apostles and prophets because they are under their ministries. Pastors need to understand that those ministries are foundational and are an asset to any ministry. Conversely, apostles and prophets cannot feel that they are "above" pastors because of the authority and anointing upon their lives. Ministries are given to work together in peace. It is with this understanding that apostles, prophets, and pastors have to work together in the local church or assembly.

APOSTLES VERSUS PROPHETS

Another reoccurring trend in the Body of Christ is apostles trying to function as prophets and prophets trying to function as apostles without the anointing or call of the Lord. Apostles will have to function sometimes as prophetic voices in the Body of Christ. However, this is not to be their area of concern. Their main job is to advance the Kingdom of God, not to be prophets.

Because some apostles have become deceived, thinking that they are all of the ministry gifts wrapped into one, they began to prophesy beyond the measure of their gifts. This turns into a soulish prophetic ministry, which usually ends up with the apostle thinking that he cannot ever be wrong. The apostle then begins to prophesy for money and personal gain. Then, the apostle usually develops a following based upon his personality rather than the person of Christ. The result is then a deceived apostle with a following of beguiled souls.

Prophets also have to guard themselves against thinking that God is going to elevate them to the apostolic office. It is true that Paul was a prophet/teacher before entering into apostolic ministry. However, this was at the call of the *Lord.* With some, God does use the prophetic office as training for the apostolic office. Many prophets, though, have taken it upon *themselves* to try to operate as apostles. They begin to start ministries and churches claiming apostolic authority and right. The result is a deceived prophet whose prophetic ministry is stifled by deception.

Though there are similarities between apostles and prophets, they must resist intruding on one another's offices based upon their own desires. In addition, apostles and prophets have to resist competing among themselves as to which office takes preeminence in the Church. The Word declares that He placed the apostles first. However, all ministries are equally important to the plan and purpose of God in the earth. No ministry is better, though functions differ. Apostles and prophets have to learn how to relate to one another through the Spirit, balanced by humility and love.

Notes:

Lesson 6 – Apostolic and Prophetic Goals

God releases the anointing to fulfill certain tasks. The Word teaches that there are differences in ministries and functions.

> **Now there are diversities of gifts, but the same Spirit. And there are differences of administrations, but the same Lord. And there are diversities of operations, but it is the same God, which worketh all in all. But the manifestation of the Spirit is given to every man to profit withal. (I Corinthians 12:4-7)**

Since there is diversity in God, we know that each ministry is designed to accomplish certain tasks. The same holds true for the apostolic ministry as well as the prophetic ministry.

In the Body of Christ, apostles and prophets are foundational ministries. In our natural bodies, the heart and the mind are foundational organs. We discover that the roles that the heart and mind play in the human body reflect the roles of the apostles along with apostolic people and prophets along with prophetic people, respectively.

FOCUS OF THE APOSTOLIC ANOINTING

The focus and thrust of apostles and apostolic people is reflective of the role of the heart in the human body. The heart is the central location for where blood is pumped to the rest of the body. It is said to house our innermost feelings and emotions.

Apostles and apostolic people endeavor to reveal to the Church the heart of God. They have a love for God and strive to make others aware of the love of God towards them. Apostles and apostolic people strive to see the Church advance in the Kingdom of God.

In the same manner that the heart pumps blood throughout the Body, they will make sure believers walk in the newness of life by their continual ministering in the Church.

Though apostles and apostolic people have a zeal for order and structure in the Church, it must be balanced by love. Apostolic individuals will know how to express the innermost heart of God and bring people into a father-child relationship with the Lord.

At its core, apostles and apostolic people want to see men and women be conformed to the likeness and image of Christ. The heart of God from the beginning was to have sons and daughters. The apostolic ministry is given to see this fulfilled in this life.

FOCUS OF PROPHETIC ANOINTING

Apostolic individuals long to see the heart of God fulfilled in having sons and daughters, while prophets and prophetic people work to see the sons and daughters fulfill the plan, purpose, and will of God. Prophetic individuals operate the same as the mind in the human body. Prophets and prophetic individuals have the responsibility to communicate the mind and thoughts of God. They will have insight into what God is saying and doing. However, they must be careful not to misinterpret the mind of God based upon their emotions and biases.

Though prophets and prophetic people are aware of the love of God, their words will immobilize people to action after the father-son relationship is established. Prophetic individuals will know how articulate the Word of the Lord and inspire others to follow His commands. God created man for His glory and to fulfill His purpose. The prophetic ministry is given to see this fulfilled in the earth.

APOSTOLIC AND PROPHETIC TOGETHER

The apostolic and prophetic anointings work together as a check and balance to one another. In the human body, the heart brings substance to what is received in the mind, while the mind filters the emotions of the heart. Apostolic ministry balances the prophetic ministry by bringing stability and order to what God is saying. Conversely, prophetic ministry balances apostolic ministry, by giving direction to what is received through the apostolic ministry.

They work together so that the Church will have the heart and mind of God in all situations. In the human body, an alert mind and strong heart provide the basis for a strong body. The same is true in the Church. The apostolic anointing and the prophetic anointing work together to ensure the Body of Christ remains strong.

QUESTIONS:

1. Discuss the focus of the apostolic anointing.
2. Discuss the focus of the prophetic anointing.
3. How do the individual goals of these ministries surface their ministries?

Notes:

Lesson 7 - Understanding Anointings

Today, believers worldwide have developed an appreciation for spiritual gifts and manifestations. However, misinterpretations of scripture have caused individuals to boast in possessing "anointings that do not exist. Before exploring the apostolic and the prophetic anointing, we must develop a clear understanding of the anointing.

Both the Old and New Testaments contain numerous references to the anointing. The anointing is an important component in the service of the Lord. Under both covenants, the servants of the Lord could not serve without it. The Hebrew and Greek terms for "to anoint" denote to smear or rub in. This implies that the anointing becomes a part of the individual who has received it.

ANOINTINGS IN THE OLD TESTAMENT

The scriptures tell us that there are diversities of anointings. This was true even under the Old Covenant. The Hebrew term for anointing was mashchah (pronounced mash-khaw'). It means a consecratory gift and also to consecrate. This implies that the anointed individuals were gifts to those they ministered to. In addition, they were set aside unto the purpose for which they were anointed. In the Old Testaments texts, God anointed individuals to perform various tasks and stand in certain offices. They were anointed stand in the offices of priest and king, through oil being poured upon them.

1. Aaron anointed as a priest

> *And thou shalt put them upon Aaron thy brother, and his sons with him; and shalt anoint them, and consecrate them, and sanctify them, that they may minister unto me in the priest's office. (Exodus 28:41)*

2. David anointed king by Samuel

> *Then Samuel took the horn of oil, and anointed him in the midst of his brethren: and the Spirit of the Lord came upon David (I Samuel 16:13a)*

In each of these examples, the anointing of God was demonstrated by a physical anointing of the individual. However, others were anointed to stand in positions of authority without an outward anointing.

1. The Judges

> *Nevertheless the Lord raised up judges, which delivered them out of the hand of those that spoiled them. (Judges 2:16)*

2. The Prophets

> *Since the day that your fathers came forth out of the land of Egypt unto this day I have even sent unto you all my servants the prophets, daily rising up early and sending them. (Jeremiah 7:25)*

It is clear that God raised up the individuals and set them aside to stand in positions of great authority without an anointing ceremony. They were anointed solely by the Spirit of God. We discover that no one could function in any of the above offices except God placed them. Though there were other individuals whom the Lord used, we find that God anointed individuals to stand as prophets, judges, priests, and kings continually.

There are also other individuals who were anointed by God to function in other capacities without an anointing for service. Individuals such as the builders of the tabernacle, the seventy elders who prophesied after receiving Moses' spirit, Barak, Ezra, Nehemiah, Zerubbabel, and various others. They received an anointing from God to accomplish specific tasks.

ANOINTINGS IN THE NEW TESTAMENT

After Christ's resurrection and the outpouring of the Spirit, we find that God still anointed individuals for service. We discover from the scriptures that men and women are anointed stand in ministry offices such as apostles, prophets, evangelists, pastors, and teachers.

> ***And he gave some, apostles; and some, prophets; and some, evangelists; and some, pastors and teachers. (Ephesians 4:11)***

Likewise, aside from functioning in ministry offices, individuals are anointed and endowed with certain gifts for Christian service. These other gifts and offices are listed in the book of I Corinthians and in the Book of Romans.

> ***But the manifestation of the Spirit is given to every man to profit withal. For to one is given by the Spirit the word of wisdom; to another the word of knowledge by the same Spirit; To another faith by the same Spirit; to another the gifts of healing by the same Spirit; To another the working of miracles; to another prophecy; to another discerning of spirits; to another divers kinds of tongues; to another the interpretation of tongues. (I Corinthians 12:7-10)***

In addition,

> ***Having then gifts differing according to the grace that is given to us, whether prophecy, let us prophesy according to the proportion of faith; Or ministry, let us wait on our ministering: or he that teacheth, on teaching; Or he that exhorteth, on exhortation: he that giveth, let him do it with simplicity; he that ruleth, with diligence; he that sheweth mercy, with cheerfulness. (Romans 12:6-8)***

Though various terms are used in the New Testament to describe the anointing of the Spirit, two terms seen frequently. The first is found in II Corinthians 2:21,

> ***Now he which stablisheth us with you in Christ, and hath anointed us, is God.***

The Greek work for anointed in this text is chrio (pronounced khree'-o). It means to be consecrated to an office or religious service. Paul used this term to express that God had placed him in the apostolic office to minister to the Church. Thus, we find that one receives an anointing to serve. Even if you are not called to a ministry office, there is an anointing on you to serve in some capacity. The second term used for anointing is found in I John 2:20,

But the anointing which ye have received of him abideth in you, and ye need not that any man teach you: but as the same anointing teacheth you of all things, and is truth, and is no lie, and even as it hath taught you, ye shall abide in him.

The Greek word used here is chrisma (pronounced khris'-mah). We derive the word charisma from this word. It is defined as the special endowment of the Holy Spirit. Hence, the anointing comes with gifts and endowments from God.

Therefore, as believers, we should consider the use of the expression, "I am anointed to do such and such" carefully. We must not confuse personal gifts and talents with the endowment of the Spirit.

When we receive the Spirit of God, its presence abides in us. The same is true for the anointing. When God places a particular anointing upon an individual, it remains. The gifts of God will operate according to the need and purpose of the moment. However, the "anointings" or endowments of the Spirit abide with an individual at all times. Even in disobedience, the anointing to be king remained upon Saul. David recognized this (I Samuel 24:6).

OFFICE VERSUS ANOINTING

The Spirit of God governs all of the spiritual activities within the Body. He anoints and appoints according to the ultimate will of the Father. Since the Body of Christ is made up of many members, there are various needs within it. The Spirit of God then anoints individuals to fulfill the needs within the Body. The greatest burden for ministry rests upon the leaders, specifically, the apostles, prophets, evangelists, pastors, and teachers. Their purpose is found in Ephesians 4:12:

1. **To perfect the saints**
2. **To train them for the work of the ministry**
3. **To build up the Church spiritually**

However, these ministries are not responsible to minister to everyone. God uses the entire Body of Christ. The members of the Body of Christ are called to minister to one another, even if they are not called to a ministry office.

> *As every man hath received the gift, even so minister the same one toward another, as good stewards over the manifold grace of God. (I Peter 4:10)*

Therefore, God anoints individuals to function in similar ways to those of the ministry offices. Believers will have anointings on their lives, which, if not careful, may be mistaken for a call to a particular ministry office. This implies that there are some that have a pastoral anointing and gift without being called to pastor a church. Moreover, there are some that have an anointing to teach without functioning in the office of a teacher. This is also true for apostles and prophets.

The underlying purpose of this lesson is designed to illustrate the difference between someone who stands in the apostolic or prophetic office and someone who has an apostolic or prophetic anointing. So that there will be no confusion. Numerous individuals today have laid claim to an apostolic or prophetic anointing without understanding all that it entails. Remember never to confuse a call to a ministry office with an anointing of the Holy Spirit.

The beginning lessons were designed to show the magnitude of the apostolic and prophetic office. It is with this understanding that we can discuss now the apostolic and prophetic anointings.

QUESTIONS:

1. **What is one of the terms used for anointing in the Old Testament?**
2. **What are two terms for anointing used in the New Testament?**
3. **Is an anointing to serve the same as a call to the ministry? Explain.**

Notes:

Lesson 8 – The Apostolic Anointing

We have learned that the apostolic ministry was displayed first in the New Testament Church. Its role in the Church has been influential from the beginning. However, everyone in the Church is not an apostle. There is diversity in the Body of Christ.

> **Now ye are the body of Christ, and members in particular. And God hath set some in the church, first apostles, secondarily prophets, thirdly teachers, after that miracles, then gifts of healings, helps, governments, diversities of tongues. Are all apostles? Are all prophets? Are all teachers? Are all workers of miracles? Have all the gifts of healing? Do all speak with tongues? Do all interpret?**
> **(I Corinthians 12:27-31)**

Paul taught that the Body of Christ was made up of many members and that each had a particular function. He explained that the Church was the same as a physical body. Since our body has many parts, then so does the Body of Christ. He concluded this portion of his argument by showing how God developed offices and gifts in the Church beginning with the apostles.

Afterwards, to further illustrate his point of diversity, he asks a series of questions to which the answer is a resounding "NO!" All are not apostles and all or not prophets, and so on. Since all are not apostles, God makes the benefit of apostolic ministry available to all by placing an apostolic anointing on other members in the Body. Those possessing an apostolic anointing are referred to as apostolic people. They have a passion for Christ and the Church and an unwavering faith in God.

CHARACTERISTICS OF APOSTOLIC PEOPLE

The apostolic anointing is as broad as the apostolic office. However, there are certain characteristics that apostolic individuals share. No matter what their individual functions are in the Church, apostolic people will exhibit the characteristics of disciples, sons, and big brothers.

Apostolic People are Disciples

1) Disciples are students and pupils.

Apostolic people have a hunger and love for the things of God. They have a passion not only to learn of Him, but also to become as He is. The Word of God has priority in their lives.

2) Disciples follow their masters whole-heartedly.

Apostolic people will follow Christ with all of their hearts. They have the ability to endure every trial and test in order to follow Him.

3) Disciples are disciplined.

Apostolic people will have a zeal for the holiness of God.

Their lives will reflect the necessary discipline and self-control needed to remain in right standing with the Lord.

4) Disciples have one goal: to become like their instructors.

Apostolic people have a desire to be like Christ. Their goal is to reflect His image in their everyday lives. They have an undying urge to bring honor and glory to the Master.

5) Disciples respect their instructors.

Apostolic people have respect for Christ and His representatives. They will respect leadership in the Church and in the government.

Apostolic People are Sons (and Daughters)

1) Sons are obedient to their parents.

Apostolic people will be true sons and daughters in ministry. Even as Timothy was a son unto Paul, they will exemplify this in their relationships with Church leadership. Not only will they be subject to leadership, but more importantly to the Word of God and the leading of His Spirit.

2) Sons reflect the image of their fathers.

Apostolic people endeavor to reflect the nature and character of Christ. They will be godly individuals reflecting the holiness of God. They follow the verse of scripture that states, "Be ye holy; for I am holy." (I Peter 1:16)

3) Sons follow in the father's footsteps.

Apostolic people believe that whatsoever things they have seen Christ do, they can do also. They will not only demonstrate the character and nature of God, but His works will follow them. They do not need a position or title, they believe because He said so. Apostolic believe unquestionably in the following scriptures,

> **And these signs shall follow them that believe; In my name shall they cast out devils; they shall speak with new tongues; They shall take up serpents; and if they drink any deadly thing, it shall not hurt them; they shall lay hands on the sick, and they shall recover. (Mark 16:17-18)**

In addition,

> **Verily, verily, I say unto you, He that believeth on me, the works that I do shall he do also; and greater works than these shall he do; because I go unto my Father. (I John 14:12)**

Apostolic People are Big Brothers (and Sisters)

1) Big brothers protect their siblings.

Apostolic people are watchful over their brothers and sisters in Christ. They will help immature and weak Christians in their walks. They believe that they are their brother's keeper. They will be sensitive to the needs of others through the Spirit.

2) Big brothers enforce their parent's rules to their siblings.

Apostolic people respect God and Church leadership. They will remind their brothers and sisters to follow the Word, the Spirit, and their leaders. They will endeavor to see others walk in obedience to Christ and leadership.

3) Big brothers earn the trust of their parents.

Apostolic people are respected by the leaders they serve under and those they serve with. Leaders will trust their advice and counsel because they do not seek to please themselves, but to please God and to serve leadership faithfully. Apostolic people will also have the respect of other members in the Body of Christ. This is due to the love and respect that they demonstrate towards Christ, leadership, and the brethren.

CHARACTER TRAITS OF APOSTOLIC PEOPLE

Because apostolic people have the favor of God, the respect of leadership, and the support of the brethren, they must strive to reflect the nature of Christ at all times and resist pride. Paul gives the necessary character traits of apostolic people in his instructions to the Roman Church (Romans 12:9-17)

1) Apostolic people have to demonstrate genuine love. They must be lovers of good and despisers of evil in all forms. (Romans 12:9)

2) Apostolic people must love the brethren and seek the welfare of others above themselves. (Romans 12:10)

3) Apostolic people have to resist procrastination and stagnation in ministry. They must maintain a zeal for the work of the Lord. (Romans 12:11)

4) Apostolic people have to be people of faith and prayer. They have to be able to endure tribulation, inspire hope in others and themselves, and be prayer warriors. (Romans 12:12)

5) Apostolic people have to be selfless. They must be willing to meet the needs of others and be easily entreated. (Romans 12:13)

6) Apostolic people should speak words that edify and build up other believers at all times. They are not to be gossips and revilers. (Romans 12:14)

7) Apostolic people have to be in tune with other members of the Body. They, through the Spirit, have to be sensitive to the failures, trials, and successes of others. (Romans 12:15)

8) Apostolic people have to be impartial in their relationships with others. They should be as God who is no respecter of persons. (Romans 12:16)

9) Apostolic people have to be harmless. They ought to be gentle, representing the nature of God in all honesty. (Romans 12:17)

Anyone who feels he/she has an apostolic anointing has to guard themselves against pride, deception, and visions of greatness. In turn, they will be pillars in the midst of the Church.

RECOGNIZING THE APOSTOLIC ANOINTING

Apostolic people will function uniquely in the Body of Christ. In order to recognize the apostolic anointing, one must first know what are the functions of apostolic individuals.

I. Apostolic people carry the Word of God. (II Timothy 2:15)

Apostolic people understand and know how to make proper application of the scriptures. They, like apostles, will understand many of the hidden things of God through scripture.

II. Apostolic people impart life into other believers. (Ephesians 4:29)

Apostolic people know how to communicate spiritual truths to help others believers grow in the knowledge of the Lord. Their words will consistently minister grace, wisdom, insight, hope, and faith to those around them.

III. Apostolic people help establish others in their walks with the Lord. (Galatians 6:1-2)

Apostolic people have the spiritual insight to help babes and immature saints gain strength in the Lord. They will help them to overcome weaknesses and sins through wise counsel, prayer, and support.

IV. Apostolic people are shameless witnesses of the Lord. (Acts 1:8)

Apostolic people are gifted to evangelize in the name of the Lord. Whether at home, at work, or out in public, they seek to win souls to the Kingdom of God. They realize that their relationship with God, not a title, compels them to witness. They do this with great conviction and results.

V. Apostolic people serve and support leadership. (Hebrews 13:17)

Apostolic people believe in divine order. They will support godly leadership without question. No matter what capacity they serve in the Church, it is done as unto the Lord and with respect unto God-given leadership. They also encourage others to follow the leadership as they follow the Lord.

VI. Apostolic people expose false doctrines and ministers. (Matthew 7:15-16)

Apostolic people exercise mature discernment. They are zealous for the Lord and the purity of the Church. They have the wisdom to recognize false ministers and doctrines readily. They are bold in identifying the false while supporting the truth.

VII. Apostolic people possess the power and gifts of the Spirit. (Mark 16:17-18)

Apostolic people have the gifts in operation in their lives. They believe God in all things. They are believers who have powerful testimonies of the power of God being displayed in their everyday lives.

Though apostolic people are scattered throughout the Body of Christ, no matter where they are, they bring life and stability among the congregation.

FLOWING IN THE APOSTOLIC ANOINTING

If you believe there is an apostolic anointing upon your life, there are certain practical steps to take to flow properly in it. Without these disciplines in your life, you will never flow fully in what God has for you.

I. Study the Word of God. (II Timothy 3:16-17)

Apostolic people have to consistently study and apply the Word of God to their lives. The Word is what will govern their hearts and minds and equip them for service in the Body of Christ.

II. Have an established prayer life. (Ephesians 6:18)

Apostolic people have to be consistent in prayer. It is the only way to remain strong in the Lord. In addition, prayer will give them greater sensitivity in the Spirit. Prayer will guide them to their rightful places in ministry.

III. Follow Leadership. (Hebrews 13:7)

Apostolic people have to be submitted to local leadership. They must follow the vision of the leaders as they follow Christ. Without being submitted to authority they will become ineffective in the Church.

Now that we have discussed the characteristics of apostolic people, the character traits of apostolic people, recognition of the apostolic anointing, and how to flow in the apostolic anointing, let us now look at the prophetic anointing.

QUESTIONS:

1. Discuss the characteristics of apostolic people.
2. What are the necessary character traits of apostolic people?
3. What do we look for to identify an apostolic anointing upon individuals?
4. What steps are needed to maintain a flow in the apostolic anointing?
5. Do you know anyone whom you would consider apostolic? Explain.

Notes:

Apostolic and Prophetic Foundations 101: Foundational Studies for the Apostolic and Prophetic Ministries

Lesson 9 – The Prophetic Anointing

Though God uses prophets, they are not the only individuals who are able to communicate the Word of the Lord. Even in the Old Testament, we discover that God wanted His Spirit to dwell in mankind that they all could know His voice and express His counsel. Moses, through prophetic insight, made this point clear to Joshua.

And Moses said unto him, Enviest thou for my sake? Would God that all the Lord's people were prophets, and that the Lord would put his spirit upon them! (Numbers 11:29)

Moses understood that God wanted all of His people to be able to speak for Him. With this in view, we find in the New Testament that God gives believers the gift of prophecy and the prophetic anointing to declare His counsel without occupying the office of the prophet. This is so the prophets will not have to do all of the prophesying and that the counsel of God will reach all believers.

CHARACTERISTICS OF PROPHETIC PEOPLE

Individuals who possess a prophetic anointing upon their lives are referred to as prophetic people. Prophetic people possess the same characteristics as the prophets. They act as messengers and interpreters, though not with the same level of influence and authority.

Prophetic People as Messengers

1) Messengers are deliverers of the sender's message (Ezekiel 3:27)

Prophetic people have the responsibility to speak the message of the Lord to others in the Body. They will do this while in subjection to the structure of the local assembly and under the supervision of leadership.

2) Messengers are responsible for the message they carry (Ezekiel 33:7)

Messengers have to be careful not to lose or damage the message given them. Some messengers have to deliver oral messages as well as written. Prophetic people are responsible for the Word that God will give them. Prophetic people have to be careful not to speak anything but what God gives them.

3) Messengers must not alter the message given (Jeremiah 23:28)

Messengers have to be careful to deliver the given message only. The messenger has to be careful not to tamper with the message in any way. Likewise, prophetic people have to deliver the Word as God gives it to them. They should not alter the message because of personal opinion/bias, popularity, or gain.

4) Messengers have to be fearless (Jeremiah 1:8)

Messengers have been killed for the message they delivered. Throughout history, there are numerous stories of messengers who are killed for relaying another's message. Therefore, a messenger has to be fearless. Prophetic people will be bold in declaring the revelation God gives them. They cannot fear rejection of man, but rather live to please God.

5) Messengers have to be trustworthy (Amos 3:7)

A messenger has to have the trust of the one who sends him. Prophetic people must have the trust of the Lord, leadership, and the brethren in order to be received properly. Prophetic people are to possess integrity. They have to be faithful to Christ and the Church.

Prophetic People as Interpreters

1) Interpreters are important to any kingdom.

Interpreters are a valuable resource to any kingdom. They provide nations with the opportunity to communicate with one another without confusion. Prophetic people help other believers to understand the move and will of God. They help individuals to apply the Word delivered by leadership.

2) Interpreters understand more than one language

Interpreters have the important task of establishing communication between people of different nationalities and languages. Prophetic people, like prophets, will be gifted to understand the different ways that God speaks. Some are able to interpret dreams and visions. Others will be able to show how everyday events speak prophetically to individuals.

3) Interpreters are skilled in communication

Interpreters are more than mere translators. It is a known fact that it is possible to lose meaning through literal translation. Therefore, it is imperative that the interpreter be able to not only translate, but also communicate the intent of the words spoken. Prophetic people have to be able to communicate the heart and mind of God as well as the Word of God.

4) Interpreters do not work alone

When an interpreter is present, he is not the primary communicator. The interpreter's function is secondary to those who are conversing, though vital. Prophetic people do not work alone. They minister in connection with other mature members and leadership to ensure the counsel of God is understood. In addition, they endeavor to see its proper application in the Church and in believers' lives.

CHARACTER TRAITS OF PROPHETIC PEOPLE

Because prophetic people have the gifts of God consistently operating in their lives, their characters have to developed and conducive to facilitating prophetic ministry.

Without character, prophetic people will become deceived, prideful, and move in a realm that is reserved only for prophets. Jesus' "Sermon on the Mount" began with what is called "The Beatitudes" **(Matthew 5:3-12)**. Prophetic people must use Jesus' words to govern their characters.

1) Blessed are the poor in spirit. Prophetic people have to be humble. Because God uses them to communicate His messages, humility will bring stability to them and protect them against deception.

2) Blessed are those who mourn. Prophetic people have to be broken before God. They should grieve over the sins of the Church and make intercession to God on behalf of the people.

3) Blessed are those who are meek. Prophetic people have to be mild-mannered and even-tempered. They cannot be governed by their emotions, nor bound by biases and anger. Though God may use them to challenge others, they have to do it in the proper spirit.

4) Blessed are those who hunger and thirst for righteousness. Prophetic people have to be holy. Their daily task is to reflect the holiness and righteousness of God in their walk with Him.

5) Blessed are those who are merciful. Prophetic people should be compassionate and forgiving. Compassion will help them to minister without condemnation, while forgiveness will keep their hearts pure toward others even in light of persecution, rejection, and misunderstanding.

6) Blessed are the pure in heart. Prophetic people must have the right motives in ministering. They do not minister for popularity or position, but because of the love of God and the brethren.

Again, if these do not govern prophetic people, they leave themselves open for a snare and trap of the devil.

IDENTIFYING THE PROPHETIC ANOINTING

Prophetic people are dispersed in the Body by the discretion of the Spirit. Some people who possess a prophetic anointing do not recognize it. To aid in the identification of the prophetic anointing, let us look at how prophetic people will function within the Body.

I. Prophetic people proclaim the Word of God. (Colossians 3:16)

Prophetic people love the written Word of God. They know how to interpret prophetically scriptures. They boldly speak the Word.

II. Prophetic people are intercessors. (Romans 15:2-3)

Prophetic people are powerful intercessors. They are instant in prayer. They know how to intercede for the people of God according to His will. They have consistent prayer lives. They take the burdens of others upon themselves to present them to God.

III. Prophetic people motivate believers to fulfill the will of God.

Prophetic people have the ability to recognize gifts and ministries in others. They help others to recognize their gifts and use them according to the will of God while respecting established leadership.

IV. Prophetic people declare the prophetic word of the Lord. (I Corinthians 14:3)

Prophetic people have the gift of prophecy. However, their prophetic words will not have the same anointing, clarity, and depth of the prophet. Their words will edify, exhort, and comfort the Body of Christ.

V. Prophetic people interpret dreams, visions, and signs. (Numbers 12:6)

Prophetic people have the ability to interpret dreams and visions. Some frequently have dreams, visions, and impressions. They are able to interpret the languages of God with success.

VI. Prophetic people expose false prophets and doctrines. (I John 4:1)

Prophetic people have the spiritual insight to recognize error. Through the revelation of the Spirit and by their knowledge of the Word, they warn others against deception and false ministry.

VII. Prophetic people have other gifts operating in them. (I Corinthians 12:11)

Along with the gift of prophecy, prophetic people have other gifts of the Spirit. Most common among them is the discerning of spirits, the interpretation of tongues, the word of knowledge, and the word of wisdom.

WALKING IN THE PROPHETIC ANOINTING

If you feel you have a prophetic anointing upon your life, it will not flourish if you are not consistent in your relationship with the Lord. The following steps are needed to walk consistently in a prophetic anointing.

I. Study the Word of God. (II Peter 1:19)

Prophetic people have to consistently study and apply the Word of God to their lives. They must remember that every prophetic word spoken must be in line with the scriptures.

II. Have an established prayer life. (Ephesians 6:18)

Prophetic people have to be consistent in prayer. It is the only way to remain strong in the Lord. Prayer is the vehicle through which prophetic words are received. Praying keeps the prophetic anointing fresh.

III. Submit to Leadership. (Hebrews 13:7)

Prophetic people have to be submitted to local leadership. They must follow the vision of the leaders as they follow Christ. Though they have prophetic insight, they are not to think they are more spiritual than leadership and other members. In order for the prophetic ministry to remain in them, they have to respect the authority that God has placed over them.

Now that we have discussed the characteristics of prophetic people, the character traits of prophetic people, identification of the prophetic anointing, and how to walk in the prophetic anointing, we will be able to recognize this anointing in the lives of others.

QUESTIONS:

1. Discuss the characteristics of prophetic people?
2. What are the necessary character traits of prophetic people?
3. What do we look for to identify a prophetic anointing upon individuals?
4. What steps are needed to maintain a flow in the prophetic anointing?
5. Do you know anyone whom you would consider prophetic? Explain.

Notes:

_____
_____
_____

About Kingdom Builders International Ministries

KBI Ministries was created as a building ministry in the Body of Christ. Even as Zerubbabel and Joshua rose up to rebuild the house of God in Jerusalem, we have the vision to build up the Kingdom of God, which is the Church. This ministry is designed to aid the local Pastor, Church Leader, Para-Church Organization, and Foreign Missions in establishing the people of God in His Kingdom. That is, to help "make ready a people for the coming of the Lord." I Peter 2:5 states that the people of God are lively stones built up to be a spiritual house, acceptable to God by Christ Jesus.

KBI Ministries is dedicated to building God a spiritual house, of believers, even as Solomon built Him a physical house. It is our desire to see the glory of God in the Church as it was in the temple that Solomon built. Our aim is to fulfill the commission given to those in ministry as outlined in Ephesians 4:12-13. This will be accomplished through proclaiming the written word of God, and also through imparting prophetic revelation to the Body of Christ; it is written, the spirit of prophecy is the testimony of Jesus.

KBI Ministries' God-given purpose is to promote Maturity, Unity, and Holiness in the New Testament believer, to call for change and repentance in the Body of Christ, to prepare a chaste bride for Christ at His coming, so that we may present to Him a Church without spot or wrinkle.

OTHER TEACHING/STUDIES FROM KINGDOM BUILDERS INTERNATIONAL MINISTRIES

Victorious Living 101: This teaching and study material is about Victorious Living through Christ. There are three areas that have to be overcome: The World, The Flesh, and The Devil. It is only then that we can live the victorious Christian life. We cannot expect to overcome the flesh, except we separate ourselves from the world. We will not defeat our adversary unless we bring the flesh under control. In addition, we will not be able to live in victory, until we overcome the devil.

Kingdom Basics 101: This teaching and study material focuses on Kingdom living. It focuses on developing character, understanding God's plan and purpose for your life and it explores the gifts and ministries of the Holy Spirit.

Apostolic and Prophetic Foundations 101: The focus of this teaching and study material is not only to bring clarity and understanding to the apostolic and prophetic offices, but also to the apostolic and prophetic anointings. These lessons will help individuals to recognize the operations of these anointings in the lives of believers.

Ministry Matters 101: This teaching and study material is designed to bring sobriety to the purpose of ministry in the Kingdom. Ministry is a valuable part of the Kingdom. God anoints individuals in the Church with ministries and gifts to glorify Him. However, as the day of the Lord hastens, we find many believers entering into ministry with wrong motives. In addition, others are pursuing gifts for their own personal gain. Learn why God gives gifts and ministries and how to avoid error.

If you would like to purchase these teaching resources, to see a full listing of music, books, and other ministry resources, and/or to learn more about Kingdom Builders International Ministries, please visit our website at www.kbpublishing.net